RESET

Classics of How to Construct a Meaningful Life and Manage Time Effectively

Raymond A. Falconer

COPYRIGHT

TABLE OF CONTENTS

INTRODUCTION

How can this help you Reconstruct a wonderful time?

The normal human life expectancy is appallingly short. Living to be 80 years of age provides you close to 672000 hours. No mystery time is possibly our most important asset. Today, a large number of us are influenced by the urge that we ought to be more helpful, more effective, or dedicate our chance to something entirely different.

Truly our focus on efficiency is inflicting considerable harm. Rather than getting to an ideal state of production, "tricks of the trade" and time utilization tactics leave us feeling concerned and hollow.

In these key chapters, you'll get notions about endlessly employing time successfully, that encourage you to renounce traditional approaches and appreciate the joy of finitude.

In the following Chapters and sections, you'll learn

- why you ought to take up a side hobby instead of a part-time employment;
- how the premodern notion of eternity affected how people expended their energies; and
- the most efficient technique to further strengthen your tarrying talents.

CHAPTER 1

TIME IS UNCONTROLLABLE

You'll always be unable to control your time.

For the great majority of mankind's collection of experiences, folks have required to be affluent with the objective that they wouldn't need to function as hard. In any way, as of late, being occupied has transformed into an encouraged life choice known as hustle. Research suggests that the wealthier you are, the more likely you are to feel restless about not having adequate chances to do everything. What's more, our entrepreneurial economy is at blame.

Private business motivates us to utilize our time, talents, and assets to get the greatest advantage. All the while, several well-off people make advancement at the usual expense for most daily goods, a major living. In the meanwhile, the gig economy has confined those less fortunate to maintain different sources of income with limited monetary stability.

Obviously, being too busy isn't everyone's concern to worry about. In any case, for us who are hooked on being filled continually with efficiency, it's time we explored this yearning.

The essential point here is: You'll always be unable to govern your time.

As a self-declared efficiency freak, the author went through years of striving to increase his time-usage talents. He acquired pricy notebooks, tried various things using tactics like arranging his day in 15-minute chunks, and divided his life into A, B, and C requirements. These tactics allowed him to feel that he was typically approaching the absolute edge of commanding his efficiency. However, the day on which he, at last, defeated his time won't ever come up.

All else being equal, he was left considerably more restless than any other time in recent memory.

On one occasion he got a revelation: his attempts to boost his time were useless. While he thought himself a valuable guy, the unpleasant fact was that the endeavors he pleased most effectively were trivial. Indeed, he could faithfully empty his inbox. However, replying to texts just generated additional messages. In the meanwhile, things that were crucial to him, such as investigating an article he planned to create, were left scattered.

The creator's experiences showed him a key illustration: the more you try to eliminate your time, the more dissatisfied, concentrated, and emptiness you feel. He calls this the Catch 22 of constraint. In any event, in truth, you'll always be unable to attain everything that you could like to. Furthermore, by embracing this truth, you may start to hone in on what makes a difference. In the creator's instance, renouncing the urge to rule time and giving up on the obscure utterly altered him. He even devoted himself to a drawn-out romance and created a family.

CHAPTER 2

THIS PRESENT TIME IS UNIQUE

Our opinions no time unlike the present are fundamentally contemporary.

If you were a laborer in early middle age England, your worries may have included widespread disease, giving installments to the Church, or doing backbreaking labour for the monarch who held the land you lived on. In any case, one challenge you could never have encountered was dealing with your time.

As a rancher, you'd have risen with the sun and dozed off in the dark. Undertakings like emptying the cows and harvesting crops would have been completed depending on the scenario. Concerning timing things? You may have claimed that an endeavor took up to a "Miserere whyle," or the time it takes to study Psalm 50 from the Bible. What's more, because ranch labor seemed infinite, there was a strong motive needed to rush to get done with a task.

The potential of finding the optimal balance between important and pleasant activities would have been unessential in middle age England. Things being what they are, our concentration on utilizing time effectively is a cutting-edge enhancement.

Here is the important message: Our perceptions no time like the present are organically current.

Part of the reason why premodern humans weren't upset about having a too limited period is that they didn't consider their lifespan confined. All things being equal, folks thought regarded their lives as a trivial prelude to eternal. So there was a strong need to agonize about what you didn't do in this lifetime. Premodern humans also would in general deem global history outdated. In some communities, people recognized that collection of experiences burnt through a few predictable phases.

This changed decisively with the rise of mainstream innovation. In the cutting edge time, people began to perceive history as continually pushing toward a glorified future. With the move from religion at the center of importance and the rise of wariness regarding the great beyond, persons began to engage themselves with maximizing their limited time on Earth.

The common notion wasn't the major variable in our cutting-edge viewpoint eventually. The growth of tickers likewise assumed a role in our cutting-edge time-related troubles. Mechanical tickers are widely thought to have been established by middle age priests who are supposed to tell the current time to recite morning requests before daybreak. In any event, clocks turned out to be notably vital throughout the enhancement of present contemporary jobs.

While laborers had always been paid for dubiously described words like "full-time employment," during the Industrial Revolution, manufacturing plant owners began paying their representatives to continue to enhance their perks. Thus, time progressively evolved from notion to asset - something to be employed instead of the substance life was composed of.

CHAPTER 3

MAXIMIZING LIMITEDNESS OF TIME

By recognizing our finitude, we may construct a fulfilling existence.

Any research into time would be fractured disregarding constructed by the German scholar Martin Heidegger. In his magnificent work of art Being and Time, Heidegger maintains that our finite human existence is constrained by time. All in all, we are confined to the time that we spend on this earth. Our finitude defines our world.

Tragically, the larger portion of us spends our efforts in getting away from or ignoring this fact. Heidegger refers to this as "falling." Some of us stay away from the idea of finitude by seeking for diversions or immersing ourselves in the tedious routine. Others find consolation with the idea that they don't need to select what to do by any length of the imagination. These folks follow a prescriptive presence by getting married or living in a spirit-obliterating stance.

So how would it be advised for you to reply to keep on with a genuine life? As emphasized by Heidegger, you need to gaze up to your barriers.

This is the important message: By recognizing our finitude, we may construct a fulfilling existence.

The acceptance that your lifetime is confined doesn't need to be a sad idea. Consistently, the modern Swedish genius Martin Hägglund loves his late spring get-away with his more remote relatives on Sweden's Baltic shore. The route into the joy Hägglund experiences on these travels is that they're limited. Since Hägglund doesn't have trust in endlessness, he recognizes that he will not have the choice to join in these expeditions for forever. His interactions with his family who depart are restricted by their mortality. And, interestingly, the beach where the get-aways occur is short due of the receding ice masses in the vicinity.

Embracing finitude needs not to be linked up with having a concentrated attitude on death. According to another perspective, it's amazing that you have any time at all. This was the type of thing that the Canadian author David Cain confessed when a mass shooting occurred on Danforth Avenue in Toronto just fourteen days after he attended an event at the spot. Cain recognized that there was no limitless regulation ensuring his endurance.

The creator doesn't spend continually pondering about his death. As to Heidegger, recognizing finitude involves knowing that each choice concerning how to organize your time needs penances. But instead of feeling heartbroken that you can't do everything, your options might represent a guarantee to choose what makes the most impact to you - whether you're renouncing various possibilities to support your family, watch twilight, or create a book.

CHAPTER 4

FOCUSING ON CLEAR GOALS

Improve as a slowpoke by concentrating on constrained goals.

Thinkers like Heidegger who have expanded on finitude will typically strive not to supply valuable ideas about spending time effectively motivated by a paranoid concern of drifting overly close to the self-improvement type. In any way, by taking into consideration Heidegger's notion that determining what we would rather not spend energy on is a center test, we may reach a few determinations. So, we want to improve on our ability to tarry.

A considerable proportion of us admonish ourselves for our inclination to dawdle. Yet, delaying is human nature and is inevitable. To turn out to be superior slowpokes now is the perfect moment to change our concentration from trying to accomplish all that to concentrating on what makes the largest difference.

The essential message here? Improve as a slacker by concentrating on narrow goals.

The fundamental guideline to improve as a slowpoke is by paying yourself first with your time. Let's imagine you have an endeavor that is crucial to you. This may be an inventive project or in any case, cultivating a connection you haven't had the energy for. Rather than sitting tight momentarily then having the chance to make it happen, effectively create time in your schedule. You may have a try at coping with a venture for the primary hour after you awaken, or arranging time in your calendar.

The succeeding guideline is constraining your works ongoing. While thinking about what you need to do, it may very well be attractive to begin a huge number of new chores. However, by having several endeavors on your plate, what will in general happen is that you bounce beginning with one and then onto the next at whatever point one venture gets hard or exhausted. Therefore, you never complete what matters quite a deal to you. Handling each project in turn leads you to break it into more modest responsibilities. On some random day, you'll merely be accomplishing a handful of tasks while stirring up your goal.

The final recommendation is to avoid second-level demands. Regardless of whether we like it, we merely lack the opportunity and determination to complete everything that we need to do.

Whether it's a kinfolk you merely to some degree enjoy or a semi-fascinating open job, figure out how to express no to a piece of the things you should perform. On the off chance that action isn't in your main five items you need to escape existence, it may very well be to your greatest benefit to stay away from it.

CHAPTER 5

THE DISTRACTIONS AROUND

There's something more to your interruptions outside what may be anticipated.

Regardless of whether you live to be 80, you will not have 672000 hours. Life is filled up with a broad variety of unplanned situations. Furthermore, we likewise will quite often get diverted.

Thinkers since the hour of the archaic Greeks have been troubled by the human tendency for disruption. Their major focus has been the fact that our existence is defined by our thought.

Obviously, obtaining full command over your consideration is inconceivable and terrible. As revealed by neuroscientists, obligatory contemplation is crucial to our endurance. It permits us to travel far distant from an impending transport. Simultaneously, to reach our aims, we actually want to dominate a precise degree of attention.

Here is the essential message: There's more going on than would be anticipated.

Today, the clearest disruptions we confront come from electronic innovations. At this point, a great number of us recognize that innovative organizations gain by capturing and tracking our consideration - and delivering our knowledge to promoters. Organizations do this with a "enticing scheme" that keeps us reliant on our displays. In any event, the danger with innovation isn't just that it burns through the time we spend on it. Web-based entertainment also contorts our vision of the globe.

Innovation affects our views about what's essential, the threats we encounter, and our political adversaries. This greatly influences how we behave unconnected. The inventor was an enthusiastic Twitter customer till he recognized that innovation was experiencing severe harm even after he'd closed down for the afternoon. After his youngster was created, he'd theorize how to describe his child's charming behavior in a tweet as opposed to treasuring minutes together.

Be that as it may, innovation alone isn't to be condemned for our predisposition to get distracted. Truly doing what makes a difference to us might create startling anxiety. In the event that you were trying to produce a novel concentrate a faraway lodge, you'd probably nevertheless track down it tough or laborious to zero in entirely on your venture. You might stay away from work with relaxation or by drifting off into a fantasy country.

The explanation why doing the task you enjoy might create difficulty is that when you concentrate on an action that really matters, it forces you to face your obstructions. You could find that you can't pull off an imaginative undertaking. Thus you will more often than not keep away from these genuine elements by yielding to distractions. By being cognizant of this difficulty, you may cope with your anxiety as opposed to submitting to each secure motive.

CHAPTER 6

ENJOY THE PRESENT MOMENT

Live for the present second as opposed to for what's to come.

Have you at any point felt that errands normally take more time than arranged? The mental researcher Douglas Hofstadter recognized this uniqueness and gave it a name: "Hofstadter's regulation." According to this law, if you try to provide yourself an additional chance to symbolize running extra time, you'll in any event wind up running throughout your new evaluated time.

Hofstadter publicized his rule to some degree sarcastically. Be that as it may, on the off chance that you've at any point attempted to design a venture, you realize its guideline will in general be valid. However, while we understand that life is in many cases beyond our control, a considerable lot of us spend our lives monotonously attempting to plan the entire time.

This is the important message: Live for the present second instead of for what's to come.

The inventor experienced childhood in a family that arrived up at the plane airport three hours ahead of time. Yet, in the end, he knew that regardless of the amount you plan, there's no promise that things would come out as you'd want. Attempting to manage the future merely swaps your strain to fretting about the subsequent month, occasion, or duty.

Over-the-top organizing isn't the primary method that we will more frequently than not live from here on out. A large number of us are powerless to anything the creator refers to as the "when-I-at long last" attitude. We let ourselves know that when we at last meet the perfect large other, handle our psychological wellbeing concerns or cope with our responsibilities, life will at long last commence. Our present second is never-ending aiming toward some idealized future condition.

Somebody living from one check to another and striving for better work isn't to be chastised for desiring a superior future for oneself. Yet, most of us may assist ourselves out by attempting to live right now as opposed to living for what's to come.

Assuming you've at any time strived to live right now, you'll realize that it's more difficult than one would imagine. In Zen and the Art of Motorcycle Maintenance, inventor Robert Pirsig discusses one image of a survey of the much-captured Crater Lake in Oregon.

Remaining before the fallen antique spring of streaming lava, Pirsig couldn't resist the chance to feel far removed from the moment. The splendor of the place is concealed by the method that it's changed into a recognized vacation resort. Accordingly, the experience of life during the period was darkened.

Rather than castigating yourself for not having the choice to engage in the present properly, try basically understanding the method that you're continually living in right now. You will fail or come up short at living right now since, regardless of whether you like it, the current second is all that exists.

CHAPTER 7

RELAX YOURSELF

Occupy side hobbies or spend energy with loved ones to obtain the pleasures of leisure time.

In his 1962 book The Decline of Pleasure, the commentator Walter Kerr recognized our increased predisposition to use our limited energy with beneficial pursuits. We party to prolong our organization or spend the end of the week at home to redecorate the house. However, gradually, we neglect to carve out the opportunity to relax.

The deterioration of relaxation was a side-effect of the Industrial Revolution. Manufacturing plant proprietors advised workers to employ their downtime in methods that would boost their productivity at work. This was, shockingly, aggravated by job reformers and association pioneers who argued that laborers would utilize their additional accessible energy to work on themselves via education or social exercises.

This concept of investing our free energy properly continues on capturing us nowadays. To reap the joy of engagement entirely, the moment has come for us to reassess our technique to deal with leisure.

The critical message here is: Take up side interests or invest energy with loved ones to receive the rewards of relaxation time.

Nowadays, indulging a side hobby might be to some degree a shame. Calling something a side interest will in general suggest that you're a beginner. It's considerably more popular to pack in a part-time job or a movement that is planned to bring benefits. Be that as it may, enjoying a side interest can enhance your life exactly because it's done basically for joy. Allowing oneself to be ordinary at anything may be liberated.

For more than twenty years, the British musician Rod Stewart has enjoyed designing a model train track of a 1940s American metropolis setting. Stewart's motivation for the project wasn't to boost his image. Also, he wasn't extremely skilled at creating models. He recruited someone to do the electrical wiring.

Side interests may enhance your experience. Be that as it may, when considering how to manage your relaxation time, you should think about investing energy with others. A concentration in Sweden discovered that higher bargains decreased at a more significant rate when more people were on vacation. All in all, Swedish individuals were the happiest when they had the option to share their downtime with others.

These findings have key repercussions for becoming a computerized traveler - the way of life when people increasingly shun stodgy workplaces to operate online firms from their PCs. While digital migrants are free to lay back in pristine regions like Thailand or Guatemala, increasingly, many are realizing that traveling alone may be lonely.

CHAPTER 8

PRACTICE-COSMIC INSIGNIFICANCE THERAPY

Instead of worrying about your life's purpose, engage in astronomical irrelevance treatment.

At some point, hovering above the American Midwest on a trip for business, the VP of a clinical equipment firm had an epiphany - that she couldn't bear her existence. Although she used to have an enthusiastic attitude on her profession, it had ceased to feel meaningful. Presently she fundamentally grabbed on to the expectation that her continuous work may trigger delight down the road.

Ending up pondering how you spend your days might be significantly irritating. In any case, it's a fundamental initial move toward building a satisfying life. Which drives us to an essential inquiry regarding using time effectively: how would we cause the time we do have to count?

The important message? Practice astronomical irrelevance treatment as opposed to agonizing over your life's motivation.

When the Covid pandemic occurred in 2020 pushing legislators throughout the globe to order lockdowns, there was a general consensus in the United States that with the harm and hardship, the pandemic was a turning point that made us pause and examine the main issue. Indeed, even the inadequate medical care systems and racial gaps that the epidemic revealed contributed to the feeling that we were, at least, being encouraged to recognize what makes the largest difference.

The trouble with trying to pin it down is that it very well may be a mainly impacted exercise. Many New Age followers agree that we're each endowed with a magnificent "life meaning." So, in the event that you're not in that frame of mind to quit your office task, you may prefer to have a major life that isn't in the cards for you. In truth, be that as it may, how you manage your time has no value according to the cosmos.

We're naturally programmed to perceive the cosmos according to our perspective. This motivates us to copy and pass forth our traits. In any case, in the terrific plan of general time, our singular lives are unimportant.

From the outset, this could appear to be a frightening thought. However, looking at this rationally, it's equally wonderfully liberated. Embracing your irrelevance lets you free from the nonsensical rules you create for yourself to make your lifetime spectacular. According to limitless irrelevance therapy, every career is substantially as useful as putting up a sustaining feast for your baby. It doesn't make any difference if you're not nearly as talented as Mozart or Albert Einstein. According to the universe, producing a book or searching for any goal that you care about is a terrific way for investing your 672000 hours.

FINAL THOUGHTS

The important message in these three points is that:

The cutting edge viewpoint of no time like the present is a fruitless quest to rule it. However, you may remove yourself from this cultural viewpoint. By working with as opposed to against your human limits like hesitation, interruption, and the capacity to live right now, you can embrace your mortality and develop a significant life.

noteworthy guidance:
Make use of technology that is dull or has a single use.

We generally succumb to the enchantment of advanced interruptions because they provide us an escape from feeling forced by our boundaries. To combat this inclination, make your mobile phone as tiring as doable by deleting each of your web-based entertainment apps and turning on the grayscale mode in your availability options. You can likewise take a stab at utilizing innovation that is intended for a solitary reason. For instance, read novels on a tablet rather than on your telephone; you'll be considerably less inclined to shift your focus.

www.ingramcontent.com/pod-product-compliance
Lightning Source LLC
La Vergne TN
LVHW020525160826
845677LV00015B/3910

9798844475696